Going Beyond the Wound

Going Beyond the Wound

A Spirituality for Men

Dennis J. Billy, C.Ss.R.

New City Press
Hyde Park, NY

Published in the United States by New City Press
202 Comforter Blvd., Hyde Park, NY 12538
www.newcitypress.com
©2018 Dennis J. Billy

Cover design by Leandro de Leon

Library of Congress Cataloging-in-Publication Data
Billy, Dennis Going Beyond the Wound — A Spirituality for Men/ by
Dennis J. Billy.
   pages cm Includes bibliographical references.
  ISBN 978-1-56548-611-9 (alk. paper) 1. Title

2017956519

ISBN: 978–1–56548–611–9

Printed in the United States of America

In glory, honor, and praise of "*Abba, Father,*"
the God of Jesus Christ

"I have been crucified with Christ;
and it is no longer I who live,
but it is Christ who lives in me."
Gal 2:19-20

Contents

Foreword

This book, a response to an invitation, also extends one. It comes from a request to speak at the National Religious Vocation Directors' Convention on "Male Spirituality." I was surprised, since I had never spoken about or written on the topic. Always one for a challenge, I put aside my apprehensions, accepted the invitation, and began putting together some ideas on what the Catholic faith offers concerning male spirituality.

As I gathered my thoughts, my mind kept returning to my father's workshop in my childhood home on Jefferson Avenue in Staten Island, New York. This workshop, the only unfinished room in our house, occupied an unassuming corner of our basement. It had a workbench with all the basic carpentry tools: a small power saw for cutting lumber; a cabinet containing oil cans, paints, and varnishes for his work; an unfinished bookcase stacked with back issues of *Popular Mechanics* and a slew of helpful do-it-yourself books; and a desk where my father planned his projects, kept all his paper work and paid the bills. I also remember him tinkering in there, building things with us for our school projects, being the person to turn to when you needed help and had to get something done. He was a "go-to" kind of dad. He was a man's man, and I am grateful he was my father.

Whenever I think of my father this basement workshop comes to mind, for it tells me something about the kind of person he was. A New York City firefighter, he had to spend many long nights away from his wife and family. At times this absence made him seem distant, a perception reinforced by his being the family disciplinarian while my mother was the nurturer and caregiver. Still, my brothers, sister, and I knew that he loved us very much and wanted only the best for us. He worked hard to provide a good education and give us everything we needed to succeed in life. What he could not buy, he built with his own hands. I have fond memories of watching him saw lumber, mix cement, lay tiles, and build fences to create enough space indoors and outdoors for his growing family. I also remember him at his desk studying for the exams required of him as a firefighter. I remember being especially proud the day he came home and announced that he had been promoted to the rank of Battalion Chief.

In my mind's eye, I often find myself in my father's workshop, either doing my homework at his desk or tinkering with his tools and building things that I hoped would make him proud of me. Even today I spend a lot of time there, that is, in my mind. Now that he's gone, it's my way of feeling close to him. To be honest, much of my life's work has been nothing more than tinkering in my father's workshop. The workbench, tools, bookcase, and desk are different, but the places they occupy in my imagination are very much the same. In this special place, I can plan things, build things, create things— and be a man's man. The chapters that follow emerged from my tinkering in the workshop of my mind, the one rooted in my father's basement workshop. I invite you, my reader, to receive what I offer on Catholic spirituality for men from the unfinished workshop in the basement of my spiritual home. May it help you reach a deeper awareness of the presence of God in your life. May it help you on your journey home.

Dennis J. Billy, C.Ss.R.
March 19, 2017
The Solemnity of St. Joseph

Introduction

Although this book is directed toward men, it has value for anyone wanting to understand his or her spiritual condition. It focuses on male spirituality from within the tradition of the Catholic faith and seeks to draw out the relationship between the two. It acknowledges the many approaches to male spirituality, some highly developed and others implicit or on the periphery of men's awareness. It understands that society often asks men to play certain roles, that many men are conditioned by their society, and that they are apt to change as society itself changes. Some of the most basic insights of the Catholic faith, however, affirm that stable characteristics of the male personality stem from human nature itself, the complementarity of the sexes, and the existential situation of living in a fallen world. As men journey through time and live out their lives, they adapt to changing cultural demands and circumstances yet remain remarkably the same. They remain stable and recognizable amid the various levels of physical, mental, spiritual, and social growth (or regression).

This book rests on the premise that men are created in the image and likeness of God, yet are deeply wounded by humanity's primal fall from grace. These touch every dimension of a man's makeup—the physical, psychological, spiritual, and communal—and affect men in unique ways. These wounds can be healed only by the redemptive love of Christ and the action of his Spirit through the life and ministry of his Body, the Church. In the person of Jesus of Nazareth God entered our world to give himself to us completely and become our nourishment and source of hope. In his passion and death on the cross Jesus embraced our wounds and healed them by the power of his resurrection. By bearing the wounds of his passion in his glorified flesh, the Risen Christ demonstrates his power over death and reminds us that our wounds—whatever they are and wherever they come from—not only can be healed, but can be transformed by the power of his love. Therefore, Catholic men are called to live in the wounds of the Risen and Glorified Christ. The Apostle Paul, one of the early Church's great men of God, wrote, "I have been crucified with Christ; and it is no longer I who live, but it is Christ who lives in me" (Gal 2:19-20).[1] Like Paul, Catholic men are called to join their wounds with those of the crucified Lord and allow the life of the Risen Christ to penetrate their lives. In this way, their wounds will be healed and their lives transformed.

The book contains five chapters. Chapter 1, "A Catholic Spirituality for Men?" defines basic terms used in the discussion. Chapter 2, "Our Wounded Selves," considers the wounds that all men share by their common humanity. Chapter 3, "The Broken World of Men", examines the wounds specific to men. Chapter 4, "Christ, the Wounded Healer," looks to Christ as the healer of humanity's wounds, with a focus on those unique to the experience of men. Chapter 5, "Living in the Wounds of the Risen Lord," shows how the transfigured wounds of Christ's resurrected life touch men's lives and carry them to the threshold of the divine. Each chapter concludes with a section entitled "Practicing Catholic Male Spirituality" and a "Prayer to Jesus" that might help in the struggle to be saintly men of God open to the promptings of the Spirit in their lives. The epilogue, "A Manifesto for Catholic Male Spirituality," sets forth general principles for Catholic men to follow in their journey of faith.

Although this book does not pretend to offer a comprehensive Catholic spirituality for men, it does identify many key characteristics that they should consider as they strive to fulfill themselves in the faith. It focuses on how Catholic

---

1 Unless otherwise stated, all Scripture quotations come from *Holy Bible: New Revised Standard Version with Apocrypha* (New York/Oxford: Oxford University Press, 1989

men can remain comfortable in their own skins yet be faithful to Christ. It looks to Christ's manhood as a key to their Catholic identity and to the wounds of the Risen Lord as the means through which their own wounds will be healed and transformed. Men must look to him for the courage to face their inner demons and persevere to their journey's end. If nothing else, this book raises Catholic men's awareness of their central role in the Church's vocation, life, mission, and well-being. It challenges men to rise to the challenge of the Catholic faith and asks them to acknowledge their wounds, entrusting them to the Risen and Glorified Lord.

1
A Catholic Spirituality for Men?

Yet among the mature we do speak wisdom, though it is not a wisdom of this age or of the rulers of this age, who are doomed to perish. But we speak God's wisdom, secret and hidden, which God decreed before the ages for our glory.

1Cor 2:6-7

Before entering a discussion about a Catholic spirituality for men, we first need to explain what we mean by "spirituality." This word has become so common that it has many possible meanings. Some definitions of "spirituality" are openly religious, others less so. Today, many distinguish between being "religious" and "spiritual." The first has to do with organized religion, while the second discounts institutional structures and focuses on the personal search for transcendence.[2] This chapter presents some definitions of spirituality then examines Christian (especially Catholic) spirituality and its relevance for men in their search for wholeness.

What is Spirituality?

One broad definition of spirituality covers almost every possible understanding of the term. "Spirituality," it says, "is the way in which a person understands and lives within his or her historical context that aspect of his or her religion, philosophy or ethic that is viewed as the loftiest, the noblest, the most calculated to lead to the fullness of the idea or perfection being sought."[3] Although it may seem academic and abstract,

---

2 See, for example, Diarmuid Ó Murchú, *Reclaiming Spirituality* (Dublin: Gill & Macmillan, 1997), vii-ix, 1-2, 27-31.

3 Walter Principe, "Toward Defining Spirituality," *Sciences religieuses/Studies in Religion* 12/2(1982): 136.

this definition makes sense in almost any circumstance. It applies to whatever religion, philosophy, or ethic a person may hold and focuses on how it is understood and lived in daily life. It also notes that "spirituality" involves more than mere intellectual knowledge, since it is also reflected in how a person enacts an ideal or seeks out perfection. A person's understanding being rooted in a given context suggests that "spirituality" is not an abstract body of knowledge unaffected by the tides of history; it operates within human culture and consciousness. This definition's weakness is its focus on the individual, making little or no allowance for communal expressions of spiritual life. In doing so, it relegates wide areas of human experience to the margins.

This understanding of "spirituality" also acknowledges three distinct levels: the experiential, the instructional, and the analytical.[4] The experiential involves what the individual or group encounters, such as a conversion experience, a prayer service, or a liturgy. The second refers to the teachings formulated from such personal or group experiences, as in a catechism or book of spiritual reading. The third touches upon the study and examination of the first two levels, for example, a scholarly article on the practices of a specific religious group or institution. These levels are distinct, but also closely related. A teaching emptied of personal experience easily becomes brittle and stale. A scholarly insight into spirituality can open up personal experience and lead to new formulations of truth. These levels of spirituality influence each other in any number of ways. How they interact reflects the overall health of a spiritual tradition.

Before moving on to a specifically "Christian spirituality," a brief look at a less academic, more popular rendering of the term might be helpful: "Spirituality is about what we do with the fire inside of us, about how we channel our *eros*. How we *do* channel it, the disciplines and habits we choose to live by,

---

4 Ibid., 135-37.

will either lead to a greater integration or disintegration within our bodies, minds, and souls, and to a greater integration in the way we are related to God, others, and the cosmic world."[5] This description of "spirituality" focuses on identifying the passion in our lives and harnessing it in constructive ways and so becoming more integrated individuals. It also emphasizes the array of relations that influence our lives and that we, in turn, can help to shape. It emphasizes the importance of channeling our inner passions to deepen our self-identity and enable us to relate to others, the world, and God in truth and love. This definition complements the first by encouraging us to ignite our inner fire so that it will blaze within our hearts and touch the hearts of the people we encounter. Jesus once said, "I came to bring fire to the earth, and how I wish it were already kindled!" (Lk 12:49). Christian spirituality is all about allowing the fire of Jesus' compassion and love to burn in our hearts.

What is Christian Spirituality?

Some years ago, wise and learned theologians debated whether there is one Christian spirituality or many.[6] Those who claimed only one said there is one Savior, one cross, one empty tomb, one resurrected Christ, one Spirit, and hence only one Christian spirituality. For them, all else was secondary and derivative. The misleading implication that following Christ involved multiple manifestations could lead to a watering down of the one gospel spirituality to which all are called. Others, however, claimed, that the Christian God was a God of variety; multiplicity and unity are not opposites, but complements. The variety of creation, full of different plants

---

5 Ronald Rolheiser, *The Holy Longing: The Search for a Christian Spirituality* (New York: Doubleday, 1999), 11.

6 For a brief outline of the debate, see Michael Heintz, "Introduction" in Louis Bouyer, *Introduction to the Spiritual Life*, trans. Mary Perkins Ryan (Notre Dame, IN: Christian Classics, 2013), 5-8. A list of participants can be found in Principe, "Toward Defining Spirituality," 127n. 3.

and animals, points to God's munificence and imaginative powers. They also point out that God is both One and Many, a Trinity of Persons—Father, Son, and Spirit— singularly one and distinctively plural. To speak, therefore, of one and many Christian spiritualties reflects God's creation, an abundance woven into the very fabric of reality itself.

Each side of this debate contains some truth. There is just one Christian spirituality. It involves following one simple rule from Christ's gospel: "If any want to become my followers, let them deny themselves and take up their cross daily and follow me" (Lk 9:23). This fundamental rule of Christian discipleship leads not only to Christ's cross and Golgotha, but also to the empty tomb. It is the cross of selfless love by which one's life is laid down for the sake of others. That is true, but many Christian spiritualities also go by many names. Some connect Christianity with a denomination such as Catholic, Anglican, Lutheran, or Methodist. Others associate it with a state of life—priestly, religious, or lay, married or single. Others identify the charism of religious orders such as Benedictine, Franciscan, Dominican, Carmelite, or Jesuit. Still others focus on certain activities, such as work, play, worship, or prayer.

For our purposes, we maintain that "Christian spirituality" is an analogous concept employed on many levels involving certain similarities and differences in its many expressions. A single Christian spirituality begets a variety of other, derivative manifestations in different times and places. What does this mean concretely? For example, Benedictine or Franciscan or Ignatian spiritualties do not replace Christ or place one interpretation of how to follow Christ on the same level as Christ himself. The many dimensions of Christian spirituality all refer to and derive their power from the person of Christ himself. This is also true for the whole of Christian spirituality, including Catholic spirituality.

What Is Catholic Spirituality?

The word "Catholic" (from the Greek word *katholikos*, "universal") points to the spread of the gospel down through history to all nations of the earth and to the farthest recesses of the human heart. It presupposes an intimate unity between the Church's structures and the spiritual lives of its members. The Church is a continuation of the mystery of the Incarnation: The Word of God, born of the Virgin Mary some 2,000 years ago, is now being born spiritually in the hearts of the faithful. Catholics believe that the Body of Christ subsists in the Catholic Church, but with varying degrees of incorporation that extend beyond its visible, institutional boundaries. Through its sacramental life this visible presence mediates the redeeming love of Christ and the sanctifying grace of the Holy Spirit to all people of good will, especially those who surrender all things to God and allow him to touch and ultimately dwell within their hearts.[7]

Catholic spirituality embodies Christian spirituality in its own way. Unlike some Protestant denominations, which in large part emphasize God's Word revealed through Scripture alone, it views Holy Writ as both revelatory and anticipatory. In Catholicism, the liturgy of the Word reveals God's will to the believing community through its various levels of meaning (both literal and spiritual), but also prepares it for the fullness of his presence in the celebration of the seven sacraments, especially in the liturgy of the Eucharist.[8] In this respect, Catholic spirituality is an intimate union of Word and sacrament. In it the risen and glorified Christ vivifies the communion of the faithful with his Spirit and in concrete, visible, palpable ways works in and through the lives of the

---

7 Second Vatican Council, *Lumen gentium* ("The Dogmatic Constitution on the Church," November 21, 1964), no. 8, http://www.vatican.va/archive/hist_councils/ii_vatican_council/documents/vat-ii_const_19641121_lumen-gentium_en.html (accessed March 25, 2015).

8 See The Pontifical Biblical Commission, *The Interpretation of the Bible in the Church* (Rome: Libreria Editrice Vaticana, 1993), 78-84, 119-21.

faithful. Sacraments are visible signs instituted by Christ, given to the Church to mediate his life-giving grace. If Christ is the Sacrament of God, then the Church is the Sacrament of Christ.[9] This sacramental principle close to the Church's heart is especially manifested in its celebration of the Eucharist, "the fount and apex of the whole Christian life."[10] For Catholics, the Church could not exist without the Eucharist, nor could the Eucharist exist without the Church.

For Catholics, the Church in all its aspects—sacramental, prophetic, institutional, communal, and mystical—is divinely instituted by Christ as a means of continuing his presence and his ministry through history.[11] Like Christ himself, the Church is both human and divine. Thus, at its core Catholic spirituality is incarnational, inseparable from the concrete, visible expression of the divine. It engages all the senses and is wary of introducing a subtle dualism by relegating God's presence to the Word alone. In a Catholic understanding, sensible reality contains traces or vestiges of God which, through the vivifying action of the Spirit, mediates the divine presence to all who believe. Like their Orthodox brothers and sisters, Catholics treasure the sensible world. Their worship engages the senses on every level—stained glass windows, candles, incense, colorful vestments, symbolic gestures, music, singing, processions—because Christ came to transform the world, both within human minds and hearts and outside of them. In Catholic spirituality, life in the Spirit is mediated through the Church to the diverse cultures, races, and ethnic groups that make it up. Created in God's image and likeness, they complement and help each other in their journey to God.

---

9 For these and other analogous uses of the term "sacrament," see Michael Schmaus, *Dogma*, vol. 5, *The Church as Sacrament* (London: Sheed and Ward, 1975), 1-19.

10 Second Vatican Council, *Lumen gentium* ("The Dogmatic Constitution on the Church," November 21, 1964), no. 11.

11 For the various models of Church life, see Avery Dulles, *Models of the Church* (Garden City, NY: Image Books, 1974), 39-108.

What Is Male Spirituality?

Talk concerning male spirituality is a relatively recent phenomenon, one that grew, at least in part, in reaction to the women's movement of the 1960s and its focus on women's unique issues and spiritual concerns. Men, however, also have unique spiritual needs rooted in their male identity and the culture in which they live. In postmodern (some would say post-Christian) Western society, men have become increasingly alienated from themselves, others, God, and the world around them. They do need help.

Men and women hold many things in common, including their fundamental spiritual needs. Men and women may not exist on different planets, as some recent literature suggests,[12] but their spiritual concerns are different enough to warrant special attention. In this light, male spirituality should not be understood as opposition to women's spirituality, but as a way of helping men discover their identity. That men and women have unique spiritual needs also belies the myth in Western society that the true self is somehow masked, even limited, by the body, which can be manipulated and altered to suit one's needs or perceptions. Human beings are embodied creatures, and so spirituality must acknowledge that men and women have differing physical needs and attributes.

At the outset, we should also acknowledge the many kinds of male spirituality, each with its own assumptions about human existence, purpose, and relationship to the world, others, and God. For example, one male spirituality may be based on the premise that God does not exist, that human beings are meant to exploit the world rather than tend it, and that from the dawn of time the relationship between men and women has been marked by the struggle for power. Another might recognize God's existence, believe that human beings are called to care for the world they inhabit, and view men

---

12 See, for example, John Gray, *Men Are from Mars, Women Are from Venus* (San Francisco: HarperCollins, 1992).

and women as a gift to each other to be appreciated, loved, and cared for. Such differing assumptions would generate differing spiritualities. If spirituality is "what we do with the fire inside of us," then all human beings are spiritual in that they act out of their inner passion. Some, however, may be more conscious of what their passion might be. Every person must face the fire being kindled within and ask whether it is burning brightly or smoldering and in danger of going out, whether they are channeling it in creative ways or allowing it to burn out of control in a way that could damage or destroy themselves and their very world.

I seek to identify the contours of an authentic Catholic spirituality for men. To do this, I must consider everything that has been said so far about spirituality in general, as well as its Christian and Catholic delineations. What is more, attention must be paid to the needs generally felt to be ingrained in men's human makeup: to lead, provide for, and protect, as well as their desire to take initiative and act in creative and constructive ways. An authentic Catholic spirituality must also encourage men in their inward journey of self-discovery. It must be rooted in the teachings of the Church and encourage men to follow Christ in a way suited to having been created in God's image and likeness. It must help men answer with satisfaction the question: What does it mean to be a man in today's world? Furthermore, it must encourage them to begin their search for holiness and wholeness. Sometimes these two terms are placed in opposition, as if holiness were somehow foreign to being fully alive. The second-century Church Father, St. Irenaeus of Lyons, said "[t]he glory of God is man fully alive."[13] If wholeness has to do with the fullness of life, then holiness leads to wholeness and, in fact, can be identified with it: without God it is impossible to be whole; holiness means being full, even overflowing with the love of God in one's heart.

---

13 Irenaeus of Lyons, Adversus Haereses, 4.20.7. See also The Catechism of the Catholic Church, no. 294, http://www.vatican.va/archive/ENG 0015/_P19.HTM.

To experience wholeness today nothing could be more satisfying and fulfilling for Catholic men than sharing in the same spirit of *communio* (communion or fellowship in English; *koinonia*, in the Greek) that imbued the life of the early Christian community (Acts 2:42). The Second Vatican Council embraced *communio*, an element of the Church's identity as the visible image of the Triune God (*Lumen gentium*, chapter 4).[14] In assisting men in their quest for wholeness, an authentic Catholic spirituality should encourage them to consider what a "spirituality of communion" might mean for them. A good place to start would be Pope St. John Paul II's description of this approach to the spiritual life:

> A spirituality of communion indicates above all the heart's contemplation of the mystery of the Trinity dwelling in us, and whose light we must also be able to see shining on the face of the brothers and sisters around us. A spirituality of communion also means an ability to think of our brothers and sisters in faith within the profound unity of the Mystical Body, and therefore as "those who are a part of me." This makes us able to share their joys and sufferings, to sense their desires and attend to their needs, to offer them deep and genuine friendship.[15]

As the above passage indicates, a spirituality of communion involves both an inward journey toward contemplating the presence of the Trinity dwelling within our hearts and an outward journey toward the reflection of that same Trinity in the world around us, especially in the faces of our brothers and sisters. In their search for an authentic spirituality, Catholic men should take these words to heart. First, however, they need to know more about their human makeup and the wounds they carry deep within.

---

14 Second Vatican Council, *Lumen gentium* ("The Dogmatic Constitution on the Church," November 21, 1964), no. 4, http://www.vatican.va/archive/hist_councils/ii_vatican_council/documents/vat-ii_const_19641121_lumen-gentium_en.html

15 John Paul II, *Novo millennio ineunte* ("Apostolic Letter on the New Millennium," January 6, 2001), no. 43, http://w2.vatican.va/content/john-paul-ii/en/apost_letters/2001/documents/hf_jp-ii_apl_20010106_ novo-millennio-ineunte.html.

Conclusion

The Church needs an authentic Catholic spirituality for men. Many seem lost and without direction, adrift in uncertainty that prevents them from embarking on the inward journey toward maturity. Left to themselves, they risk drowning in cultural relativism and self-indulgence. They may become numb to their need for wholeness and lose themselves in an unending quest for mere material goods and superficial satisfactions.

Many men do not go to church because they feel out of place, ill-at-ease, as if they don't belong. Many also feel they receive little or nothing from a Church they perceive as a demanding taskmaster that imposes impossibly heavy burdens. Why even try if, at the very outset, a man feels the cards are stacked against him and he is bound to fail? The Church needs to change this perception and welcome men into full participation in ministry, life, and worship. It needs to find new and creative ways of accompanying them on their journey, of meeting men where they are and helping them find the next step to wholeness and holiness.

Such a spirituality must be rooted in love for Christ and his Church. It should encourage men to celebrate the gift of life and to mark those moments when they take ownership of their journey and share their experience with others. It needs to help them find ways, rooted in love, of relating to themselves, women, other men, God, and the world around them and so build up the kingdom of God in their midst. Most of all, it should help them embrace a spirituality of communion by which they can experience the many levels of authentic Christian fellowship. This spirituality of communion enables men to face their wounds and human brokenness and surrender to the Risen and Glorified Lord. Only the Lord himself can heal their wounded selves.

Practicing Catholic Male Spirituality

Take time to ponder your life's journey. Find a quiet place where you can reflect upon where you have been, where you are now, and where you are going. Get settled and rest in the silence. Then ask yourself some questions. What gets you out of bed in the morning? What are you passionate about? Who or what do you love most in life? If it helps, jot down three or four sentences that describe your spirituality. Be honest. Write what you truly believe expresses your deepest desires. Begin with the phrase, "My spirituality..." After writing this description, ask yourself: where does God fit into the picture? Christianity? Catholicism? The Church? Do you believe in God? Do you believe in Jesus? Do you consider yourself a committed Catholic? How do you practice your faith? What are your strengths? Where do you need to improve? What actions flow from your faith? Do they confirm and verify your faith? How do others perceive you? How do you perceive yourself? How does God perceive you?

Prayer to Jesus

Lord, to you I entrust my entire life. Teach me how to pray. Help me share my innermost thoughts and feelings with you. Deepen my love for you. Reveal yourself to me. Come and show me the way. Help me to be more aware of your presence in my life. Open my mind and heart. Purify them! Enlighten them! Enflame them! Help me to put the needs of others before my own. Teach me how to love. Help me to give, as well as receive. Help me to be a man of God and a man for others. Deepen my love for your Body, the Church. Help me walk the walk. Bridge the gap between who I am and who I would like to become. Show me the way to holiness. Make me a servant, a true disciple, a saint. Help me to put my hand to the plow and not look back.

2

Our Wounded Selves

And since they did not see fit to acknowledge God, God gave them up to a debased mind and to things that should not be done.

Rom 1:28

Catholic men must root their spirituality in a sound understanding of the human person that acknowledges what applies to all human beings as well as what impacts men in unique ways. Each of these aspects of human existence has relevance for our discussion of male spirituality and will help shape our outlook on a Catholic spirituality for men. What follows are highlights of some important characteristics of human makeup.

What Is Common to Everyone

The apostle Paul's presentation of the human person as body, soul, and spirit offers a point of departure for understanding the various dimensions of human existence: "May the God of peace himself sanctify you entirely; and may your spirit and soul and body be kept sound and blameless at the coming of our Lord Jesus Christ". (1 Th 5:23-24).[16] Paul's understanding of the human person, one of the earliest anthropologies of the New Testament, provides insight into the multifaceted dimensions of human existence.

For Paul, "body" (*soma*) refers to corporeal human existence, not in any denigrated sense (as when he contrasts "spirit" [*pneuma*] with "flesh" [*sarx*]), but as a neutral, albeit

---

16 For an analysis of this body/soul/spirit anthropology, see Henri de Lubac, *Theology in History*, trans. Anne Englund Nash (San Francisco: Ignatius Press, 1996), 117–220.

28

essential, element of human existence. Although under the sway of "law of the flesh" (*sarx*), that part of the person has been, is, and will be redeemed by those living according in the Spirit of Christ. A Christian anthropology that overlooks, disdains, or overly spiritualizes this crucial aspect of human existence lapses into Cartesian minimalism, which reduces the body to the level of a mere machine and identifies the human person with the "ghost." that lives within it.

"Soul" (*psyche*) refers to the psychological level of human existence. Here, reason, memory, the imagination, and the emotions play active roles in constructing the images and concepts upon which a positive theology of God is based. Although an authentic Christian anthropology embraces the psychological and gives a valued place to the classical traditional aspects of the soul (the rational, irascible, and concupiscible), it must not overemphasize them to the exclusion of other dimensions of our human constitution. The conscious and unconscious psychological elements interrelate in a way that preserves the mysterious makeup of the individual yet roots him or her in the larger collective whole. Each human soul, in other words, is unique and its rational and affective characteristics distinguish it from the rest of creation and mark it as undeniably human. In this respect, it images the mystery of the Triune God who, as the mystery of love itself, encompasses both one and many.

"Spirit" (*pneuma*) names the dimension of the human person open to the divine presence and awake to God's Spirit. It is the aspect of the person (the deepest part of the soul, if you will) that communes with God beneath the sphere of human consciousness and from the depths of the human heart cries out, "Abba, Father" (Rom 8:15). In the Christian tradition, spirit is the level of human existence that in contemplative prayer yearns for the direct experience of God. It has a central role in helping a person to live in communion with God. In its active dimension, it has a vital, directive, and animating influence over a person's entire human makeup. In its passive dimension, it allows receptivity and openness to the Spirit of God. In each individual, "Spirit" reflects the passive and active dimensions within the Godhead and the active and passive complementarity ingrained in the human species itself. Without this spiritual dimension of human existence, a Christian anthropology would be impoverished and would convey a hollow, superficial understanding of what it means to be created in the image and likeness of God.

As developed above, Paul's anthropology should also be considered in conjunction with his understanding of the Church as "The Body of Christ" (Eph 1:23; Col 1:18). Borrowed in part from the Platonic parallel of the human soul as "writ large" in the fabric of human society, the tripartite Pauline division translates into the Spirit, Christ as the head of the Church, and the faithful who form the members of his Body. Here, another dimension of the Pauline anthropology highlights the fundamental communal orientation of each level of human existence. This is to say, the contemplative, mental, and physical levels of human existence reach their fullest expression only to the extent that they are done "in Christ" and, hence, in solidarity with all those who, in varying degrees, are incorporated into his Body, the Church.

What Impacts Men

While the physical, the psychological, the spiritual, and the communal dimensions of human existence pertain to all human beings, the opening chapters of Genesis emphasize the complementary nature of human existence, which impacts humans in different ways.

The first chapter speaks of the creation of human beings in the image of God and the complementary nature of man and woman: "So God created humankind in his image, in the image of God he created them; male and female he created them" (Gn 1:27). In one sense, this verse refers to all human beings, since everyone is created in the image of God as either man or woman. In another sense, however, it reminds us that there are two distinct ways of being human in the world—male and female—and that, together, they reveal something of what it means to be created in God's image.

Similarly, the second chapter of Genesis speaks of the intimate relationship between man and woman: "So the Lord God caused a deep sleep to fall upon the man, and he slept; then he took one of his ribs and closed up its place with flesh. And the rib that the Lord God had taken from man he made into a woman and brought her to the man" (Gn 2:21-22). Man and woman, in other words, made from the same substance, are made for each other. These verses and those immediately following describe what this complementary relationship entails. Woman comes from deep within man. The rib from which she is formed shows that she is bone of his bones and flesh of his flesh (Gn 2:23). It represents the part of man that expands and contracts as, in-and-out, he breathes his life-giving breath. It also lies close to his heart. The verse tells us that woman was made for man, and that he sees her as someone both distinct from himself, yet also an intimate part of himself.

Woman, moreover, is taken from man's unconscious self while he was in a deep sleep. She touches something deep within him and reveals to him something about himself of which he normally is not aware. Here, we can learn something from the Jungian insight that all human beings represent a combination of the masculine (*animus*) and feminine (*anima*), men typically being conscious of the former and unconscious of the latter, while with women it is normally the reverse.[17] In this respect, women help men achieve wholeness by helping them in a process of individuation by which they become more and more conscious of their inner feminine, while men do the same for women by helping them get in touch with the unconscious, masculine side of their personalities.

---

17 See, for example, Wallace B. Clift, *Jung and Christianity: The Challenge of Reconciliation* (New York: Crossroad, 1985), 21–23; Pat Collins, *Intimacy and the Hungers of the Heart* (Dublin: The Columba Press, 1991), 102.

Woman is also depicted as a gift of God to man. Earlier in the chapter, the Lord God says, "It is not good that the man should be alone; I will make him a helper as his partner" (Gn 2:18). God states his intention, fashions woman from man's very flesh, and brings her to him (Gn 2:18-22). He gives her to man as a partner and helper so that he will not be alone. Woman, these verses tell us, is a gift freely given to man and so should be cherished. This gift of woman to man tells us that love involves both giving and receiving: woman is given to man and receives love in return; man, in turn, gives himself to woman and receives from her a remedy for his aloneness and a deeper understanding of himself.

Finally, the gift of woman also empowers man to leave his parents and start his own family. She gives him the confidence to step out on his own path through life with a family to lead, protect, and provide for. Man clings to his wife and the two become one flesh (Gn 2:24). Their love for one another is pure and innocent. They stand naked before one another and feel no shame (Gn 2:25). They can bare their souls to one another, without needing to hide behind clever masks or sophisticated ruses. They stand in right relationship with one another because they stand in right relationship with their Lord God. Things go awry only when they deviate from God's will by breaking his law and deciding for themselves what is good and what is evil (Gn 3:4-7).

Taken together, the common aspects of human existence shared by everyone and those that have specific effects on men and women form a complex, multifaceted, unified, profound, even mystical Christian anthropology. Although humanity's fall from grace seriously damaged these fundamental dimensions of human existence, they are in the process of being healed and elevated through the sacrificial self-offering of Christ and the transforming power of his Holy Spirit. We typically experience ourselves as both fallen and redeemed. At this point of our discussion of male spirituality, we should therefore explore how humanity's fall from grace affected these dimensions of human makeup and how Christ's redemptive action and the transforming power of his Spirit are restoring them.

Our Wounded Selves

Reflecting on the biblical account of humanity's fall from grace, the Church teaches that the sin of Adam and Eve wounded our human nature but did not corrupt it. We cannot know exactly what took place at the dawn of human history, but we do have a deep intuition that our present condition is not how God intended us to be. The sin connected to our human origins has affected us on each of the anthropological levels outlined in the previous section. Let us first look at how this original sin affects those anthropological dimensions.

After humanity's fall from grace, we lost our original continuity with ourselves, others, the rest of creation, and especially God. In the material dimension, we began to experience the hardship of labor, sickness, disease, and ultimately death itself. Prior to the Fall, we lived in a state of harmony with our bodies and with our physical nature. After the Fall, our bodies lost their orderly relationship with our anthropological makeup. We began to live in tension with our bodily nature; we began to feel ashamed of our bodies and fearful of our own mortality. The specter of death began to haunt our conscious and unconscious selves. Rather than relishing our bodily existence and rendering glory to God through it, we used it to gratify ourselves and hide from our deeper psychological, spiritual, and social wounds.

In addition to these bodily wounds, humanity's original fall from grace also affected the various powers of the soul: the rational, irascible, and concupiscible. Our powers of reasoning were weakened and our moral sense dimmed. Our hearts became divided and our wills faint. Our memory and imagination fell into disarray, while our passions became wild and unruly. We felt divided within ourselves and alienated from our truest, deepest selves. Worst of all, we used these powers, senses, and passions to distance ourselves even further from God. We began to doubt his existence. We made ourselves the measure of truth and decided for ourselves what was upright and what was not. We blessed our divided hearts and took pleasure in forbidden fruits.

The most damaging result of humanity's fall from grace was the loss of our relationship with God. In the story of the Fall, after they ate the forbidden fruit Adam and Eve hid from God. They did not understand that hiding from God was impossible; eventually he would find them and learn what they had done. This disruption of the divine-human relationship took place especially on the level of spirit, the deepest, most intimate dimension of the human person that yearns for God and is open to self-transcendence. From humanity's point of view the loving and open relationship between God and humanity was irreparably damaged and could be corrected only by divine initiative. Left to itself, humanity would be locked within its own self-centeredness. It would forever be trying to use apparent goods and superficial pleasures to fill an emptiness deep within that only God himself can satisfy.

The account of humanity's fall from grace extends far beyond the story of Adam and Eve. In the later chapters of Genesis, the stories of Cain and Abel (Gn 4:1-16), Lamech (Gn 4:23-24), Noah (Gn 6-8), and the tower of Babel (Gn 11:1-9) depict a world where the social fabric is shredding and humanity is mired in wickedness of every kind. Original sin spins ever wider and locks humankind in a spiral of evil. Everyone lives in suspicion and looks upon other people as a threat. Humanity's earthly heritage has become not love, but hatred. Human beings place their faith in false gods and follow rules of their own making. Humanity places false hope in its own resiliency and capacity for progress. The world God made has become deeply wounded as original sin spreads out from humanity and reverberates throughout creation.

The destructive effects of our original choice of sin over God touch not only our common anthropological dimensions, but also our circumstances, especially the complementary relationship between man and woman. The Genesis account describes the Fall as the source of deep-seated tension between the sexes. Tempted by the serpent, Eve beguiles Adam with the promise of becoming like God. Adam eats the forbidden fruit which Eve herself had tasted. When their eyes are opened, they have lost their innocence, no longer able to bear each other's nakedness. This shame of their bodily nature reveals their embarrassment in being fully present to one another and a growing mutual suspicion. Man blames woman for his disobedience (Gn 3: 12) and begins to rule over her (Gn 3:16). Their relationship will be forever strained, having lost their paradisal innocence and been cast out of Eden.

Even more important for our present discussion is the rupture in the relationship between the masculine (*animus*) and feminine (*anima*) within each human being. The account in Genesis suggests that the feminine comes from deep within man. Because this is so, the deeply personal and intimate relationship between man and his inner, unconscious feminine (*anima*) and the one between woman and her inner, unconscious masculine (*animus*) were damaged because of the Fall. An authentic Catholic spirituality for men must acknowledge how the complementarity of men and women presents the image of God. This is to say that each person—man or woman—not only images God in himself or herself, but also in his or her relationship with the other sex, especially in the bond of matrimony, where the two become one flesh. In this respect, their imaging of God both together and alone reflects how "the one and the many" operate within the Godhead itself.

What is more, damage to this relationship between the masculine (*animus*) and feminine (*anima*) may present itself within each person with varied intensities; in some cases it may become inverted. From this perspective, men and women who have same-sex attraction may be demonstrating one form of a common human ailment resulting from original sin. Like all fallen human beings, they need the redemption made possible for us by Christ Jesus.

Conclusion

One fundamental insight of the Catholic faith is that Jesus Christ became human to heal our broken humanity. For us, Christ entered our world, gave of himself completely to become nourishment and a source of hope. His redemptive action extends to us all, on every level of our human makeup: our common physical, psychological, spiritual, and social makeup, as well as our individual circumstances. To our wounded humanity, he offers God's compassionate love and merciful hope. If we turn to him with humble hearts, God's Spirit will work deep within our disordered selves, mending our bones, healing our wounds, breathing new life into our souls, and making us one.

Christianity proclaims that God has sent his Son into the world to heal our wounds and transform us into a new humanity. We need only place ourselves at the feet of the Lord Jesus Christ, the New Adam, who through his Incarnation and paschal mystery has overcome the power of death. He alone can heal our bodily, emotional, mental, spiritual, and social wounds. He alone can undo the sin we have inherited, as well as the personal and social, structural sins that echo our original fall from grace. He alone can liberate us, reconnect us with ourselves, with others, and with the divine. He himself will set us in right relationship with ourselves, others, the rest of creation, and ultimately with himself.

God became one of us to offer us a share in his divine life. This simple statement reminds us that God became man to initiate a new creation, to transform our broken humanity from the inside out. Jesus Christ, the Prince of Peace and the Lord of History, has come to save us from ourselves and elevate us to a higher plane. He has come not only to forgive us our sins and heal us, but also to divinize us. We all must ask this fundamental question: do we believe in his selfless and compassionate love for us? The entire discussion concerning male spirituality hinges on one simple question: "Do you believe?" Yes or no. In the end, the most important distinction is not whether we live or die, but whether we are living in Christ. This insight goes to the heart of what it means to be a Christian.

Jesus is the source of all healing. No one and no thing—abstract theory, magical remedy, or cleverly concocted myth—can take his place. He is the Son of God, the Word-made-flesh, the Savior of the world. In him lies all our hope. He alone can heal our wounded souls and make us whole.

Practicing Catholic Male Spirituality

Take a look at yourself and write some things down. Examine the various aspects of your human makeup, those you share with everyone and those specific to your male identity. How do you reflect God's image in your life? How could you reflect that image more clearly? What are your wounds? How have they affected you? How do you suffer in your body? In your mind and heart? In your spirit? How are you wounded in your relationships? Do you make friends easily? Are you able to build sturdy, lasting bonds? How do you relate to women? Do you treat them with respect or do you look upon them as objects? Are you in touch with your feelings? Can you articulate them well? Are you in touch with your feminine side? Do you hide from it, deny it, or pretend it is not there? Is it integrated into your male identity? Take a few moments and gather your wounds together. Try to identify the ones that threaten you most and that you wish to change. Prioritize them, if you wish. Which wound would you place at the top of your list? Which would you like to bring to the Lord first? Which do you feel you need to focus on the most?

Prayer to Jesus

Lord, my wounds are many. I am divided within myself and in my relations with others. I am pulled in different directions and am not sure where I should walk. I am not the man I want to be. My physical powers are no longer what they were. My mind is feeble and my will is weak. My passions are unruly and disorderly. I have lost touch with my spirit—and with you. Your image lies within me but is so difficult to discern. I feel at war with myself and, at times, even with the world. I find myself constantly placing my will before your own. I have lost touch with the gentle, compassionate side of myself. I am even embarrassed by it and hide from it. I am not an integrated person, but a man of unresolved contradictions, many of which I project onto others. Help me, Lord. Help me. I entrust myself to your benevolent and watchful care. Only you can heal me.

3

The Broken World of Men

Now the works of the flesh are obvious: fornication, impurity,
licentiousness, idolatry, sorcery, enmities, strife, jealousy, anger,
quarrels, dissensions, factions, envy, drunkenness, carousing,
and things like these. I am warning you, as I warned you before:
those who do such things will not inherit the kingdom of God.

Gal 5:19-21

Let us now interpret men and their lives from within the
Catholic tradition. Their experience may be viewed from two
perspectives. First, we can examine what they share with all
human beings; then we can look at what impacts them as men.
Men's lives, in other words, are rooted both in the experience
of their common humanity and in their experience of simply
being men. They are wounded due to humanity's original fall
from grace and by the way that wound has affected the masculine identity. Although related, these two perspectives have
distinct characteristics that affect men.

What Is Common to Everyone

All human beings, including men, are born into a broken
world and suffer the effect of the evil that entered the world
because of original sin. To some, such a claim may seem an-
tiquated and out of touch with the worldview of the secular
West. For Catholics, however, it highlights many intuitions
that touch fundamental aspects of the faith.

For one thing, the Catholic doctrine of original sin highlights the near-universal sense that in this present life things
have somehow gone awry; they are not as they should be.[18]

---

18 See *The Catechism of the Catholic Church*, nos. 396-421, http://www.vatican.va/
archive/ ENG0015/_INDEX.HTM.

We have a vague recollection of having existed in a pristine state and a nostalgic memory that we once existed in a better time that somehow has been lost. The ancients explained their experience as a series of devolutions from a golden age to the silver, to the bronze, to their present state. Modern sensibilities have inverted that sense of devolution, turning it into a process of continual progress and evolution, and in the postmodern perspective that concept has been deconstructed into a reality of competing relativities. Catholics, however, still speak of sin that humankind can trace to our origins and thereby maintain belief in the goodness of God while acknowledging the persistence of evil in a world that is fundamentally good.

This wound from the dawn of time has brought suffering not only to humanity, but also to all of creation. Because humankind is the summit of God's creation, the choice for evil made by the first man and woman has echoed throughout the universe. These repercussions are manifested in several concrete ways, and can be understood especially if we think of humanity as a microcosm of the universe. We still experience the results of this fall from grace:

+ We have lost God's friendship.
+ We feel alienated from ourselves, others, and creation.
+ Our minds have become enfeebled.
+ Our wills have been weakened.
+ Our passions and emotions have become disordered.
+ We experience work as a burden.
+ We become ill and suffer disease of every kind.
+ We diminish over time and age without grace.
+ We fear death and dread its coming.

While everyone shares in these effects, they touch men in a unique way. They experience these wounds through a man's eyes, in a man's skin, and through a man's outlook. Men's experience—and women's too—must be taken seriously. They must confront their wounds, name them, and seek to deal with them constructively to bring about healing in their lives. Catholics believe that, in the end, a man's healing will come about through the mediation of Christ and his Body, the Church. For this to happen, however, each man must acknowledge his wounds, embrace them, and present them humbly before the Lord.[19]

What Impacts Men

Men experience all the repercussions of the original sin that has shaken every person's inner life and external relations with others, indeed, with all of creation. An authentic Catholic spirituality must help men identify these profound wounds and become aware of them in their lives. These wounds touch men on every anthropological level. What follows is a description of these wounds and men's experience of them.

The Father-Wound. Many recent books on male spirituality have focused on the so-called "father-wound."[20] Although women also suffer from troubled relationships with their fathers, this wound has a strong, sometimes devastating effect on men. Typically, the father-wound is presented as a deep tension within the male psyche resulting from not having a strong father image during a man's early childhood and adolescence. This absence reverberates throughout a man's being and makes him feel unloved, unworthy of attention, and incapable of meeting the demands and expectations of his father. Men with a poor self-image often project this lack of acceptance onto their relationships with others. If not resolved, it

19 For more on humanity's original wound, see Benedict J. Groeschel, *Healing the Original Wound: Reflections on the Full Meaning of Salvation* (Ann Arbor, MI: Servant Publications, 1993), 15-42.

20 See, for example, Gordon Dalbey, *Sons of the Father: Healing the Father-Wound in Men Today* (Folsom, CA: Civitas Press, 2011); *Healing the Masculine Soul: How God Restores Men to Real Manhood* (Nashville, TN: W Publishing Group, 2003).

can manifest itself in unhealthy, even destructive ways. To one degree or another, all men experience the father-wound and may reveal it by being distant and out of touch with themselves and their emotions. This loss of contact with themselves causes a fear of intimacy with other people (especially their wives and children); if not addressed, it can make them a danger to those around them. Thus, men often feel uncomfortable exploring their inner lives and use outside activities to cope with the absence of a strong father figure. They become, in effect, the kind of men their fathers were: distant, detached, uninvolved, emotionally illiterate. The father-wound diminishes a man's ability to relate to himself, others, society, and even God. Many of society's ills stem from this wound.

This brief description of a trait common to men does not identify its cause. It arises not from a father's absence to his son in his childhood, youth, and growth to manhood (which is merely a symptom), but from something deeper, something rooted in a man's spirit. This deep, spiritual wound reveals damage to a man's psyche and personal makeup, but even more a dysfunctional relationship with the divine. The mythic, symbolic account of the Fall in Genesis chapter 3 describes what men experience deep within themselves: estrangement from God's fatherly love. In their willful decision to eat from the fruit of the tree of the knowledge of good and evil to become like God, men have turned away from God and lost touch with the meaning of life. Adam's disobedience, a refusal to listen to God in the depths of his soul, ruptures his relationship with the divine and constrains his communion with himself and others.

This deeply ingrained experience cuts men off from the source of life itself and causes estrangement on many levels. The father-wound is rooted in the loss of relationship with God. As the Apostle Paul eloquently points out, from deep within himself a man's spirit yearns to cry out "Abba! Father!" (Rom 8:15). In Adam's sin, man lost this capacity to walk in fellowship with God his Father. The primal human sin has estranged him from God. It took the coming of the New Adam, Christ, to make things right. In this light, we can discern the origins of the father-wound in a refusal of God's fatherly love and guidance. Humanity's primal alienation from the divine has deep repercussions on a man's ability to think, choose, feel, and relate to himself and others.

The Brother-Wound. One of the effects of the father-wound is a man's inability to relate in healthy and constructive ways to other men. Because they have lost their relationship with God their Father as well as with genuine father figures who image God's fatherly love to them, men pit themselves against one another, vying for attention they never had. Starving for recognition, they find it by excelling in what they do and, when necessary, holding others down to rise to the top. This desire to be noticed generates competition with other men to stand out from the crowd and draw the attention of others. Although the arenas for this struggle may differ—business, politics, sports, even scholarly and artistic pursuits—men view each other as competitors against whom they guard themselves lest they be taken advantage of and be put at the back of the pack or at the bottom of the heap.

The brother-wound is exemplified in Genesis, chapter 4—the story of Cain and Abel (Gn 4:1-16). After the Fall, humanity is left to toil and sweat. Cain, Adam's and Eve's firstborn, was a farmer; Abel, Cain's younger brother, was a shepherd. Each offers a sacrifice to gain favor with God: Cain, the fruit of his harvest; Abel, a firstling from his flock. Abel's sacrifice finds favor with God, but Cain's does not. Rather than offering another sacrifice to rectify his relationship with God, Cain lashes out in anger and kills his brother. When God asks about his brother's whereabouts, Cain responds, "I do not know; am I my brother's keeper?" (Gn 4:9). But God, hearing his brother's blood crying out from the ground, upbraids Cain for his horrible crime. God says that the ground will no longer bear fruit and banishes Cain to wander the earth. Cain becomes a fugitive, escaping death at the hands of others only by a special mark God places on him.

This first fratricide shows how the desire to gain a father's favor—in this case God himself—turns deadly. Rather than affirming his brother and nurturing fellowship with him, Cain rises up and in cold blood kills him. This violent act stems from the existential dissonance that Cain shares with all human beings because of humanity's fall from grace. But it also demonstrates Cain's deliberate choice to act on an evil inclination. By killing his brother, Cain mistakes an apparent good for a real good, distances himself further from God, and becomes an exile in his own land and among his own people. The brother-wound separates men from each other by making them suspect each other as a threat. It also divides them from God, their Father, and from the land itself, the dust from which they came and to which they will return.

The Spirit-Wound. In addition to the father-wound and the brother-wound, men also experience a wound deep in their spirits. This injury stems from disruption in their image of their maker. In chapter 2 Genesis states: "So God created humankind in his image, in the image of God he created them; male and female he created them" (Gn 2:27). Original sin so tarnishes this image that it no longer clearly reflects the divine light. Their complementary nature disrupted, man and woman no longer live in harmony. They struggle with each other for power. Having become aware of their nakedness they hide from God when he calls them (Gn 3:7-8). Sex, originally a way of expressing love, becomes a lure used for manipulation. Because of their physical strength, men dominate women in patriarchal structures instead of caring for them, who are part of their very selves.

The tension between men and women, however, stems from something much deeper and less obvious. Humanity reflects the image of God in two ways: together (through the complementarity of men and women), and as individuals (through the reflection of the masculine [*animus*] and feminine [*anima*] within each human being). The spirit-wound reveals the disruption of these complementary aspects within fallen humanity. Men have lost touch with the feminine (*anima*) side of themselves; women, their *animus*. Having lost contact with this essential dimension of their human makeup, men search for it outside of themselves, especially in their attraction to women. At the same time, they do not take responsibility for their actions, often blaming their troubles on women (Gn 3:12).

At its deepest level, the spirit-wound closes up the depths of man's being, making him incapable of intimate relationships— with himself, other men, women, and even God. Man, created to walk in God's presence and share fellowship with him, hides and fears confronting the naked truth about himself (Gn 3:8). Instead, he masks his identity and hides from others out of fear of rejection. Being cast out of the Garden of Eden represents man's incapacity to share in God's friendship. Once radically open to God, man's capacity for intimacy and friendship is now closed. The embers of his spirit grow cold and dim, and he cannot fan them to their former warmth and intensity. His spirit is dying, and he has lost touch with the divine.

The Communal-Wound. Because of the Fall, men are wounded within themselves, in their personal relationships, and in their social interactions. They place their own interests above the common good and use the public square to advance their private interests, especially pleasure, possessions, and power. Some view society as a threat to their personal freedoms; others, as an all-purpose remedy to cure humanity's wounds; still others, as an end in itself and the means by which humanity perpetuates itself. The communal-wound leaves no place within the City of Man for the City of God. Original sin does inevitably lead to personal sin, but also to social sin. Societal injustice flourishes as racial prejudice and class distinction that overwhelm communities with violence and unrest. Men band together to protect themselves from other men. Nations, cultures, even religions sometimes do the same. Society is beleaguered by endless rancor, enmity, and injustice, driven by a primal desire for self-transcendence without recourse to God.

We see how evil spins out of control after the Fall in the Genesis story of the Tower of Babel (Gn 11:1-9). At one time, when there was only one language on the earth, the human community learned how to build houses with bitumen for mortar and brick for stone. In time, to make a name for themselves and not be scattered across the earth, the people decided to build a city and a tower whose top would pierce the heavens. Building such a tower symbolizes humanity's desire for immortality. But God intervenes by confusing their tongues with different languages, forcing them to abandon their plans. The evil in this story stems not from humanity's inability to work together, but from their desire to reach the heavens, another reference to the original sin of the human desire to become like God (see Gn 3:4).

This is but one of many accounts in the early chapters of Genesis that depict how, after the sin of Adam and Eve, evil spiraled wider and wider, infecting human relationships, personal as well as social. The story of the Tower of Babel relates to the experience of men, who traditionally have had a strong affinity for building and planning, and for powerful communication. On one level, the story explains how diverse languages came to be; on another it demonstrates the danger of overreaching and the true place of human beings in God's plan.

Conclusion

An authentic Catholic spirituality for men must acknowledge the wounds all human beings suffer, as well as those unique to men's experience. It must touch men where they are most wounded and need healing. At the same time, wounds must not be imposed by suggesting to men what their own experience has been or still is. We can only present suggestions that might, in varying degrees, resonate with their experience. Men must do this work themselves. Only by getting in touch with the wounds in their everyday lives can they confront them, name them, embrace them as their own, and bring them to God for healing. Such is their task. The Church seeks to help them carry it out.

Catholics believe that only God can heal our wounded natures and forgive the injuries we inflict on ourselves and others. We further believe that God chose to do this by entering our world and becoming one of us in all things but sin. Jesus Christ, the Word of God made flesh, experienced every dimension of what it means to be human, what it means to be a man. Moreover, through his Incarnation and paschal mystery he took upon himself all our sins, embraced our wounds, and offered us a pathway to wholeness. These doctrinal and spiritual truths give shape to an authentic Catholic spirituality for men. Without them, we risk wandering off the path that leads to the Father into a hostile and inhospitable land of subjective relativities. Only Jesus is "the way and the truth and the life" (Jn 14:6).

We turn to Jesus because we believe that no one goes to the Father except through him. He alone can heal the wounds that all human beings share. He alone offers the fullness of life. He alone leads to the Father, calls men his brothers, heals their broken spirits and relationships, and calls them to communion. A Catholic spirituality for men recognizes Jesus as the one sent by God to make all things new. He is the Second Adam. Through his passion, death, and resurrection he ushered in a new creation. Men have an important role in this new world. They are called to be Jesus followers, sent to herald on this earth a kingdom not of this world. Jesus lays out a direction for men to follow. He calls them not only to discipleship, but also to friendship. He promises to accompany them as they follow him in carrying their cross. Through discipleship and friendship with Christ their wounds will be transformed and they themselves will be made whole.

Practicing Catholic Male Spirituality

Take a good hard look at yourself in a mirror. Do you see the wounds outlined in this chapter? Which of the wounds all men share affect you most? Which do you find yourself thinking about? Which accompany you throughout the day? Which ones haunt you subconsciously? Which ones follow you in your dreams? To what extent have you experienced the father-wound? How do your relationships reflect this wound? How does it color your relationship with God? Do you feel embarrassed to call God, "Abba, Father"? What about the brother-wound? Do you see other men as your competitors? If so, what are you competing for? Do you feel wounded in the spirit? How is this wound manifested in your life? Do you have a restless spirit? Have you lost your inner peace? Do you want it back? Do you long for it? How about your communal wound? Do you feel alienated from others? Do you feel isolated and alone? Do your relationships reflect self-centeredness or the love of God? Do you feel trapped by human society? How do you share in the wounded world of men? How have these wounds shaped you as a person? Has anything good come from them?

Prayer to Jesus

Dear Lord, I hear so many conflicting voices. Some tell me I must be invulnerable, a rugged individual who needs help from no one and who can shoulder his responsibilities all by himself. Others are more honest about what I can and cannot do. They tell me to let go of my need to control and to be more trusting of others. Still others send confusing messages about my role in life, telling me to meet everyone else's expectations—in society, community, workplace, family—except my own. When I look inside, I see a confusion of dreams, expectations, strengths, and weaknesses. Help me sort through these contrary voices and listen to you, the one voice that matters. Help me to acknowledge the wounds of my manhood, no matter their source. Help me place my life in your hands. I do not want to be my own man. I want only to be your disciple. Help me find my way to you and follow your voice wherever it leads.

4

Christ, The Wounded Healer

He himself bore our sins in his body on the cross, so that, free
from sins, we might live for righteousness; by his wounds you
have been healed.

1Pt 2:24

Catholics believe that through his passion, death, and
resurrection, Christ liberated humanity from sin and death
and continues living out his paschal mystery through his
mystical body, the Church. Christ and his Church form
the heart of the Gospel and so must be at the center of an
authentic spirituality for men. Christ, the wounded healer,[21]
heals the wounds men share with all human beings as well
as the wounds they share as men. He does so through the
ministry of his Body, the Church.

Christ, Healer of Humanity's Wounds

St. Athanasius of Alexandria (295-373), Doctor of the
Church and great defender of Nicene orthodoxy, wrote: "God
became human so that humanity might become divine."[22] He
meant that in Jesus of Nazareth God became a man to heal
humanity's wounds and elevate every person to new heights.
The Greek doctrine of divinization (*theosis*) names God's desire to enter intimate communion with us by making us par-
takers in his divine nature. God accomplished this through
his divine humility: he entered our world and became one of
us, gave himself completely to us through his passion, death,
and resurrection, and became our nourishment, our source

21 The term "wounded healer" comes from Henri Nouwen and Roel de Jong, *The
Wounded Healer: Ministry in Contemporary Society* (Garden City: Doubleday, 1972).
22 Athanasius of Alexandria, *De incarnatione* 54.3 (*SC* 199:458-59; *PG* 25:191-920.
See also Gregory of Nyssa, *De opificio hominis* 16 (*SC* 6:151-61; *PG* 44: 178-88).

of hope. This "soteriological principle," as it is called, suggests that God loves us so much that he not only heals our wounds but exalts and glorifies us. He does so through divine self-emptying (*kenosis*), whereby he does not grasp his divinity, but instead pours himself into our humanity out of love for us and love for his Father (see Phil 2:5-11).

"Let the same mind be in you that was in Christ Jesus" (Phil 2:5). The Apostle Paul exhorts us to put on the mind of Christ and to adopt the same humble attitude he exhibited in the Incarnation and the paschal mystery. We do so not through our own efforts, but through the gift of his Spirit, who enables us to share in the divine life and empowers us to live as adopted sons and daughters of God. If Christ has redeemed us by his Incarnation and paschal mystery, his Holy Spirit sanctifies us by dwelling in our hearts and prompting us to lead lives of holiness. Christ's Spirit, the lifeblood of his Body, the Church, comes to us through the proclamation of God's Word, and especially through sacraments, visible signs of invisible grace. These inspired words and outward signs are Christ's redeeming love acting in us. Through them, Christ breaks open our hearts and sheds upon us the light of divine love:

• He reestablishes our friendship with God.

• He heals our relationship with ourselves, others, and creation.

• He renews our minds.

• He strengthens our wills.

• He orders our passions and emotions.

• He helps us find meaning and joy in our work.

• He accompanies us in suffering and in due time heals us.

• He is present at all stages of our lives.

• He gives us the courage to face death and look beyond it.

Jesus Christ is the New Adam, the firstborn of the new creation. By taking on our wounded humanity and by hanging on the cross, he opened the heavens and allowed divine light to penetrate again the dark recesses of the human heart. Through his Incarnation, passion, death, and resurrection, the spark of divine love has been rekindled in our hearts and our wounded humanity placed on the road to recovery. Jesus's love for us, however, does not stop there: he promises not only to heal our wounds, but also to share his divinity. He does so by raising us above our earthly horizons and inviting us into intimate fellowship with the divine. Although this invitation extends to everyone, it manifests itself to men and women differently because of their specific needs and complementary natures. God always meets people where they are, and gives them more. He enters the world of men and promises to heal the wounds that impact them as men.[23]

Christ, Healer of Men's Wounds

Men suffer from a number of wounds that affect them as men. Although these wounds have multiple sources—society, culture, family, disposition, personal choice—they ultimately arise from our broken humanity, manifested in all human beings, especially in the complementary sexual relationship between men and women. Men look to Jesus as a wounded healer who can make whole every level of their human makeup, including those things pertaining specifically to manhood. Jesus teaches men how to relate to God as Father, how to relate to one another as brothers, how to befriend their inner spirits, and how to work together to build the kingdom of God.

God, Our Father. Jesus called God, "Abba," the Aramaic term of affection that in English would translate into something like "Papa." In the Jewish culture of Jesus's day it was uncommon to address God in such intimate terms, since the Lord God was considered so holy and transcendent that his name could not even be uttered. In the Hebrew tradition, the

---

23 For more on Christ's role in healing our original wound, see Groeschel, *Healing the Original Wound*, 69-100.

Lord God had many faces. At different moments, he revealed himself as a warrior king, a jealous lover, an exacting judge, a vengeful enforcer, a faithful spouse—and not only these.

Although over time God revealed himself in myriad ways (and almost exclusively in masculine terms), Christians believe that the fullness of his self-revelation came in the person of Jesus Christ. This is why the way Jesus himself addressed God was significant and eventually became normative. Because Jesus referred to God as "Abba, Father," his followers have always done the same. Of course, addressing God as "Abba, Father" cannot capture God's full identity. To be sure, reflection on Jesus's own identity eventually led the Church to understand that God is a Holy Trinity—Father, Son, and Spirit—an intimate communion of persons acting and existing as one. Even though no name or title can capture the nature of the Godhead, the Christian tradition holds certain ones in high esteem, "Abba, Father" being the highest.

"The Father and I are one" (Jn 10:30). Jesus had an intimate relationship with the Father that no one else—not even the prophets—could claim. He emptied himself and laid down his life to reestablish humanity's relationship with the Father. Everything he did was focused on this goal. He entered our world, gave of himself completely, became nourishment, a source of hope to all because he wanted us to share again in the intimacy with the Father lost through humanity's fall from grace. Thus, Jesus is the healer of our Father-wound. Because of him, we once again can turn to God and with his Spirit dwelling in our hearts cry out "Abba, Father" (Rom 8:15). Because of him, we know that the Father-wound lies deeper than the dysfunctional relationship we may have had with our own fathers or the way fathers are socialized to be distant from their sons and not relate to them emotionally or in other meaningful ways. By revealing the face of God and teaching us to address him as Father, Jesus shows that God alone can heal our brokenness, our deep human wounds.

Jesus heals our Father-wound. Because his relationship to the Father is deep and strong and intimate he can share it without diminishing his sonship. Because of him, God looks upon each man as an adoptive son.

Jesus, Our Brother. Jesus not only closes the rift between broken humanity and our Father in heaven, but also teaches men how to relate to one another as brothers. He shares with us his divine sonship and mends the broken relationship between Cain and Abel, the first brothers to appear in sacred scripture, who symbolize the fragile fraternal bond. Through his passion, death, and resurrection, Jesus demonstrates that jealousy, hatred, even death itself can be overcome by love. He shows that we were not meant to live in constant competition with other men, suspicious of their motives and afraid that they might beat us down or dominate us. He teaches that we were meant to live in fellowship, that the Father's love extends to everyone, and that we become ourselves by living for others and laying down our lives for them in our ordinary daily activities.

Jesus was an only child, but had many brothers. It is significant that the first men he called to follow him as disciples—Peter and Andrew, James and John—were brothers; and among this small band of brothers he planted the seeds of the kingdom. Jesus's mission on earth was to transform our relationship with God and the bonds we share with one another. He is the eternal Son of the Father and our first and eldest brother. He looks out for us and pursues our well-being. He heals our deep brother-wound and shows us how to forge bonds of fellowship with other men. He helps us recognize our sensitive, vulnerable side and overcome our fear of being misunderstood when we express our feelings. He also shows us how to overcome our fears of standing firm in our witness to truth. Through Jesus, our brother-wound has been cleaned and cauterized, soothed and salved, dressed and cared for; we have been transfigured and made whole. He shares his intimacy with God and allows us to partake in his divine sonship. By teaching us to address God as "Abba, Father" and to make his prayer, the Lord's Prayer, our own, he reminds us that we are members of God's family and that, as men, we are called to love each other as brothers.

Jesus came into the world to redeem humanity's brokenness and heal the festering wounds that make people lash out with hate or violence. For men, this means sharing in a relationship with him so we can see other men not as threats but treasures, not as rivals but friends, not as competitors but fellow disciples and followers of Christ. It takes courage to drop our nets and follow him without counting the cost. To do so, we must let down our guard, open our hearts to Jesus, show him how we really are, and allow his Spirit to perform his quiet work within us. To do so, we must follow him day by day, step by step, breath by breath. To do so, we must look to him always, seek forgiveness when it is called for, and live in hope. We are not doomed to follow in the footsteps of Cain, condemned after killing his brother to wander the earth, a stranger to all and a friend to none. Jesus entered our world to show us another way. By following in his footsteps, he leads us to fellowship and authentic human community. He will not mark our heads with a sign of estrangement, but bless us with the sign of his cross, look upon us as fellow sons of the Father, and guide us toward authentic human brotherhood. He came to light a fire on the earth, one that promises to burn brightly within us, warming our hearts and purifying our wounds. He mends our brokenness, making us whole.

Jesus's Healing Spirit. Jesus also came to heal our broken spirits. Our fall from grace alienated us from God and from the deepest level of our own beings. Original sin disrupted our intimacy with God, ending our capacity to walk in fellowship with him. No longer could our spirits enjoy communion with the divine. Cast out of our earthly paradise, we lived as orphans in a cruel and harsh environment. By our collective fall from grace we have lost touch with the Spirit of God. We continued breathing the air around us, but our spirits could no longer inhale and exhale the gift of divine love. As a result, our spirits became withered, deadened to the divine life for which they were made. Something had to be done for us, for we could not rectify our situation ourselves. Without that intervention, we would have remained prisoners of our own self-centeredness, forever out of touch with our true purpose.

By his passion, death, and resurrection Jesus gives new life to the human spirit. This life comes to us through the sacrament of Baptism, which immerses us in Christ's saving mysteries and restores our ability to commune with God. Because of the power of Christ's paschal mystery manifested through it, the Holy Spirit now bears witness with our spirits that we are children of God and communes with our spirits to cry out, "Abba, Father" (Rom 8:15-16). What is more, the Spirit helps us in our weakness, "for we do not know how to pray as we ought, but that very Spirit intercedes with sighs too deep for words" (Rom 8:26). The Spirit of God heals our spirit-wound and empowers us to live in Christ as adopted sons of the Father.

Healing our human spirit lets the rupture between our masculine (*animus*) and feminine (*anima*) give way to a process of integration that will make us whole. Through the power of Christ's Spirit and through Christ's paschal mystery, the image of God within, once disfigured by sin, is restored, surpassing even its original beauty. As a result, the Spirit's grace allows us to befriend our feminine side without fear of feeling overwhelmed or misunderstood. It also enables us to cast aside the false masks of masculinity (bullying, machismo, false bravado) that conceal the men God has called us to become. By healing our spirit-wound, the Holy Spirit enables us to become ourselves in faith, fully alive for God. This healing also helps us relate to women with respect and dignity. Since men's feminine side is enriched by women, men no longer consider them as objects of desire to possess or manipulate.

What is more, no longer estranged from their feminine side but integrated with it as originally intended, men no longer need to seek merely momentary gratification, forbidden pleasures that only serve to deepen estrangement from self, others, and God.

Jesus's Community of Love. Jesus calls us to communion—with God, and with each other. By his passion, death, and resurrection he transforms the City of Man into the City of God, establishing God's reign in our hearts through the power of love. This love subsists in the community of believers, which continues to live his paschal mystery. The Church is the body of the Glorified and Risen Lord living through the centuries. Mary, the Mother of Christ, is also the Mother of his Body, the Church. Her humble *fiat* represents the "Yes" of faith at the heart of the community of believers. By the Holy Spirit she conceived and in her womb bore Christ. That same Spirit is the lifeblood of the Church that affirms the "Yes" of faith, gives birth to Christ in the hearts of the faithful, manifests his love, and carries his message to the ends of the earth.

Because the Word of God became man, he speaks to men in a special way. He promises to heal the communal-wound by transforming our awkwardness in relating and inability to live with one another in harmony into bonds of fellowship and mutual trust. Through the power of his Spirit, he empowers us to live for others. He inspires us to dismantle the walls of envy, suspicion, and hatred and so build a vibrant community of love centered entirely on his life and message. He helps us understand that we have no need to erect monuments to our self-importance (veritable Towers of Babel, if you will), since God himself has opened the heavens and through the mystery of the Incarnation come into our very midst. By the power of his Spirit, Jesus Christ, "Emmanuel, God with us" (Mt 1:23), has come from heaven to live among us and dwell in our hearts. He heals our communal-wound by showing us how to enter into communion with God and one another. He imparts the same spirit of fellowship (*koinonia*) that at

Pentecost permeated the nascent Christian community in the upper room, encouraging us to place love as the central, dynamic force within society and culture.

Jesus entered our world so we can commune with God. Out of his love for us and for his Father in heaven he became one of us, gave himself to us completely, became nourishment and a source of hope. If we walk down the path of discipleship, open our hearts to him, and allow his Spirit to dwell within us, he promises to heal men's communal-wounds. Jesus, the Prince of Peace, promises to lead us away from the darkness and violence in our hearts manifested in dissonant and dysfunctional ways on every level of society: families, associations, local communities, religious and ethnic groups, national and international communities. He reminds us that humanity is not made for egoism, self-serving ideologies, and unbridled competition, but for living for others, serving the common good, and centering all social endeavors upon the dignity of the human person. By his paschal mystery, Jesus opens a way to share in a transformed humanity, whose wounds are healed and who is transformed in the glory of the crucified and Risen Lord.

Conclusion

Christ, the wounded healer, unleashes the power of love amidst our broken humanity. He heals and makes us whole because in the depths of his own humanity he has embraced our wounds, mingled them with his divinity, and transformed them into something glorious by offering them to his Father in heaven. Christ entered our world, lived among us, ministered to us, took our sins upon himself, and laid down his life—all out of love for us. He himself says, "No one has greater love than this, to lay down one's life for one's friends" (Jn 15:13). The image of Jesus as the wounded healer reveals how God loves humanity. The resurrected Lord bears the wounds of his passion and death, and promises that our own wounds, marks of great suffering, will be transfigured into deep joy.

Jesus, the wounded healer, identifies with humanity's wounds, those clearly visible as well as those hidden within our hearts. He cleanses those wounds, anoints them, dresses them, and heals them. He does so by embracing them and taking them upon himself. What is more, his healing hand touches men's lives in concrete ways. Jesus heals our *father-wound* by sending his Spirit to commune with our spirits so we cry out, "Abba, Father." He also heals our *brother-wound* by embracing us as a brother, showing us how to overcome our mutual suspicion and mistrust and helping us cultivate bonds of fellowship and friendship. He heals our *spirit-wound* by connecting us with our feminine (*anima*) side, enabling us to befriend it rather than be threatened by it, to integrate it in our lives rather than repress it. Finally, he heals our *communal-wound* by reminding us that the Kingdom of God is in our midst yet still to come, and that on earth society is called to reflect the values for which he suffered and died. Because these wounds are interrelated, healing them usually is gradual and simultaneous. In the end, Jesus's healing hand touches our hearts, deeper than the wounds themselves, enabling us to view them in a new way.

By accepting Christ's friendship and becoming his disciples, we become more and more like him. Because his Spirit dwells in our hearts, we begin to think and feel as he does. Like him, we desire to do only the will of the Father. Like him, we seek to enter the world of those around us, giving ourselves to them to become nourishment and a source of hope. Like him, we too become healers, our wounds transformed into instruments of grace. Like him, we witness the power of love to change people's lives and make them fully alive for the glory of God. Like him, our wounds become symbols of hope, signs of resurrection and witnesses to the transforming power of God's love.

Practicing Catholic Male Spirituality

Light a candle before a crucifix where you can quietly gaze upon it and ponder Jesus's significance for your life. As you look at it, ponder his wounds and place yours in them. Renew your act of faith that Jesus died on the cross for the sins of the world, particularly for your sins. Look at his bloodied body as a source of healing. Bring to him your wounds —all of them—those everyone shares by our common humanity, and those that are your own by your male identity. If it helps, write them all down. Prioritize them, if you like. List those that trouble you the most and those you find especially burdensome. Once you have finished, place your list at the foot of the crucifix or, better yet, burn them in a candle's flame. Then look at Jesus's face; see in his wounded body the source of all healing that will give you the fullness of life. Look to him as your Wounded Healer who will cure your infirmities, those that every person has, those that only men have, and those peculiarly your own.

Prayer to Jesus

Jesus, you are my Wounded Healer. Burdened by the wounds of my humanity, my male identity, and my own person, I turn to you. I place my wounds before your bloodied body, knowing that you died for my sins and the sins of all humanity. Forgive me, Lord. Heal me. Cure my innumerable wounds. Take them into yourself and over them spread the balm of your compassionate love. Help me to know you, to love you, and to serve you. Help me to become the person you desire me to be. Meet me where I am, in my brokenness. Take my hand in yours. Show me your path and help me to walk it. I cannot do it on my own, Lord. Left to myself I will remain imprisoned by my wounds and turned in upon myself. Only you can pull me out of the dark spiral in which I find myself. Only you can heal me. Only you can save me. You are my only hope. I love you, Lord. Help me to love you more.

5
Living in the Wounds
of the Risen Lord

I have been crucified with Christ; and it is no longer I who live,
but it is Christ who lives in me.

Gal 2:19-20

Jesus, the Wounded Healer, is also the Risen Lord. The
wounds he bore in his passion and death have been transformed by the power of the Father's love. Resurrected, he
still bears these wounds, but now they are signs of the love
in God's heart rather than the hatred in men's souls. Out of
love for humanity Jesus suffered these wounds. Their transformation gives meaning to our suffering and points to our hope
in the life to come. Death could not divide the bond of love
between Jesus and his Father in heaven. Nor will it defeat us,
if only we believe in him and allow his Spirit to dwell in our
hearts. This bond of love will carry us through life and beyond
death. It lies at the heart of a Catholic spirituality for men.

The Wounds of Christ

Every man could profit from a brief meditation on the
wounds caused by the instruments of Christ's passion: his
lacerated back from the scourging at the pillar, his aching and
bleeding head from the crown of thorns placed there to mock
him, the gaping wounds in his hands and feet from the nails
that fastened him to the cross, and his side and heart pierced
by a lance. These marks represent more than the brutality of
the Roman soldiers who inflicted them or the insensitivity of
the crowd that called for his crucifixion. They also stand for
the sins of humanity and their deadly consequences: our dis-

tance from the rest of creation, our alienation from ourselves, the breakdown of the human community, the anxiety and distress stemming from our estrangement from God, and much more. Jesus entered our world to save us from ourselves and to rescue us from the power of death. He gave his life so that we could have life to the full. His wounds recall his love for us and our indebtedness to him. Each of them reveals something specific about what it means to live in the wounds of the Risen Lord. Each tells us something important about being fully alive with the love of God.

Jesus's Scourging. Before the crucifixion, Pontius Pilate ordered Jesus scourged. Although the gospels do not record the number of lashes he received, Jewish law prescribed thirty-nine as a disciplinary measure to take the place of capital punishment. The soldiers conducting the scourging may have inflicted more in disdain of Mosaic code or to abuse someone they thought had defied Roman authority. In any case, the flogging tested his strength to the limit. It could have killed him had not the soldiers wanted to keep him alive to inflict yet more pain. Worse yet, scourging was administered to the back so the victim could not see what was coming; the suffering would have proved even more harrowing. Even if the lashes were applied consistently and methodically, the uncertainty of when and where the next stroke would fall heightened the pain.

Spiritual writers often suggest that readers liken the lashes Jesus received to the punishment we deserve for our sins.[24] We have escaped such cruel, excruciating suffering because he has freely chosen to stand in our place. Jesus, we might say, literally "has our back." He takes what we deserve, without complaint or second thoughts. He even takes on our unex-

---

24 See, for example, Alphonsus de Liguori, *Considerations on the Passion of Jesus Christ*, vol. 5 in *The Complete Ascetical Works of St. Alphonsus de Liguori*, ed. Eugene Grimm (Brooklyn/St. Louis/Toronto: Redemptorist Fathers, 1927), 256-58. Volume 5 consists of meditations on the passion and, at various points, focuses on each of the wounds Jesus received.

pected hardships, the ones that, like the lashes of his scourging, we can sense but do not see coming. Men's burdens and responsibilities often wear them down. Jesus does not want us to face such hardships alone. He has our backs and watches out for us. If we fall (as often happens), he takes our sins upon himself and through his suffering extends the Father's mercy. We need only seek his forgiveness with a sincere and humble heart. Jesus, our true brother, knows us through and through yet shows his love by laying down his life for us. He asks only that we love him in return by loving one another, especially by watching each other's backs. We have helped place those stripes on his back. Now transformed, they remind us of our own past and of the way of the cross that ultimately leads to the empty tomb.

Jesus's Crown of Thorns. After the scourging, the soldiers dressed Jesus in royal purple, crowned him with thorns, struck his head with a reed, and mocked him, "Hail, King of the Jews." When they had finished, they stripped off the purple cloak, replaced his own clothes, and led him out to be crucified (see Mk 15:16-20). By turning Jesus into a laughing-stock, the soldiers stripped him of human dignity. The thorns in his head represent the psychological pain and suffering that intensified his physical torture and death. He is made to feel like a non-person, as if he were a delusional fanatic, a feeble threat to the Roman and Jewish authorities. His crown of thorns also signifies the mental torment that weighed upon him and penetrated him to his core. It also suggests the wounds men suffer whenever they are mocked for daring to dream great things or instill hope in those who suffer life's heavy burdens. Jesus's crown represents humanity's battered mind, darkened reason, weakened will, wandering imagination, and saddened memory.

That crown of thorns exposes the inescapable wounds we carry within. Spoiled by bad habits and weak dispositions, our minds are full of unruly thoughts that confuse our capacity to see the truth and pursue it. Many of our wounds affect the way we think and what we seek. Our self-image and our relationship (or lack thereof) with God and others can be shaped by subliminal thoughts that remind us of our failure to live up to other people's expectations and urge us to succeed through ruthless competition for their approval and affection. We secretly yearn to be kings and princes, yet find ourselves mocked or scorned for expressing our desire to stand out from the crowd or do something extraordinary. We often become our own enemies by focusing on goals that cannot satisfy our deepest yearnings. When we fail to reach them, we turn to tactics more cowardly than kingly, fueled more by fear and insecurity than by love and its manifold fruits.

We can place our hope only in Jesus, the Wounded Healer, who has embraced our wounds, made them his own, and transformed them into living symbols of his victory over death. In his risen life, the wounds remain on his head and on his hands, feet, and side. They are not marks of shame and derision, however, but reminders that by way of the empty tomb, the way of the cross leads to new life.

Jesus Nailed to the Cross. The nails that held Jesus fast to the cross are the starkest reminders of his horrible death. The soldiers fixed him to the wooden crossbeam and upright by pounding spikes through his hands and feet, a clear sign of the brutal and violent way the Romans subjugated the peoples and nations they conquered. Jesus once walked throughout Judea laying his hands on countless people who sought relief from their physical, mental, and spiritual ailments. Now he was paralyzed, unable to touch anyone. Unlike the paralytic of the gospels, however, he was not laid out on a mat or bed of straw, but left hanging on a wooden gibbet designed to bring about a slow, tortuous death.

Losing our hands or feet would dehumanize us. Our hands enable us to interact with our environment and shape it to fit our needs. Our feet allow us to move about, to visit the world around us and explore its hidden treasures. Our hands and feet allow us to shape our societies. Not having them would limit our capacity to build, provide, protect, and create. Men who lose limbs in war suffer not only physical wounds, but also challenges to their psychological well-being and self-worth. A man without a limb (especially without hands or feet) can seem only half a man.

The marks in Jesus's hands and feet are ours, those others have caused us and those we have inflicted, whose ugly effects reverberate in our hearts. In his Incarnation Jesus has taken our wounded nature upon himself, in his suffering and death healed it, and in his resurrection transformed it. He has transformed the tree of the cross into the tree of life, and his pierced hands and feet into symbols of new life. In their glorified, risen state, Jesus's hands and feet have been freed from the cross and from the boundaries of time and space. His healing hands extend through history and can touch crowds that dwarf those who followed him when he walked the earth. His feet now take him down the corridors of time and enable him, through the members of his mystical body, to reach far-flung corners of the earth. They also enable him to accompany us on our journey through life, through death, and into eternal life. When men live in the wounds of the Risen Lord, they use their hands and feet to new purpose. They extend their hands in friendship, stretching them toward others in a welcoming embrace; they walk with others in their journey through life, accompanying them in their challenges. They use their hands and feet to build the kingdom of God and to carry his message to the ends of the earth.

Jesus's Pierced Side. To hasten the deaths of the two thieves crucified with Jesus, the Roman soldiers broke their legs. Seeing that Jesus had already given up his spirit they pierced his side with a lance. Down through the centuries, in the blood and water that immediately flowed from Jesus's side Christians have seen the blood of the Lamb sacrificed for the salvation of the world, and the water of the Spirit, the source of all grace and holiness. The blood and water, therefore, point to the sacraments of Eucharist and Baptism. The world's redemption and humanity's sanctification, in other words, flow from Jesus's broken and wounded heart.

In Jesus's day, as now, the heart powerfully represented a person's deepest convictions, those that elicited deep-seated emotions centered on what a person most loved. A stony heart was one that had lost contact with the living God, while a heart of flesh could enter an intimate personal relation with the Lord of Life. Through his suffering and death, Jesus opened humanity's heart to God and made it capable of communing once more with his Spirit. Because of Jesus, God could dwell once more in the human heart, and ours could dwell in his. The heart of the Risen Lord is both wounded and glorious. The lance that pierced his side penetrated his humanity and brushed the threshold of his divinity, opening a channel for grace to pour into the world and transform the human heart.

For most men, life's journey involves getting in touch with the heart and listening to what it says. As important as it is, a man's action in the external world often leaves him unable to understand the inner ways of the heart. Men are often out of touch with their feelings and emotions. They find it difficult to express themselves in moments of intimacy and tenderness. They can easily project their affections onto external people or objects rather than taking the time to name them, confront them, and tame them. Jesus came to change all that. In his resurrection, his deeply wounded pierced heart is transformed into a sacred heart. He looks into the hearts of men and invites us to come to him, turn our hearts to him, place our wounds into his wounded heart, be transformed by him, rest in him. His heart is large and strong enough to bear all our heartaches. By resting in Jesus's heart, we can learn to be men of heart. If we allow his Spirit to kindle a fire of love within our hearts, that fire will blaze within us and light up the world around us.

Jesus's Hidden Wound

In addition to the visible wounds on his back, head, hands, feet, and side, Jesus also suffered from a wound not visible, but that likely caused his death. A person hanging from a cross usually died not from the effects of extreme physical abuse, but from asphyxiation. To breathe, Jesus had to push up from his feet nailed to the cross and fill his lungs as much as he could. Repeating this process of pushing up from below and taking in from above, Jesus weakened from loss of blood. Each breath became more and more difficult. As his strength waned, his lungs filled with fluid. In time, they filled, and he could no longer take in the precious breath of life. The only sign of this hidden wound was the water that flowed from his side when one of the soldiers thrust a lance through his lungs and into his heart: the blood flowed from his heart, while the water flowed from his pierced lungs.

The Judeo-Christian tradition associates "spirit" closely with wind, air, and breath. Jesus's hidden wound, his struggle to take in air, represents our inability to breathe in the Spirit of God, to have fellowship with God as we once did. In his passion and death, Jesus embraced our spirit-wound and made it his own. He did so by entering our world, embracing our human condition, and taking our sinful condition upon himself. In suffering with us and taking our wounded spirits into himself, he made it possible for us to enter once more into an intimate friendship with God, a mutual indwelling and mingling of spirits. At the moment of his death, when he says, "Father, into your hands I commend my spirit" (Lk 23:46), Jesus commends into the Father's care not only his spirit, but ours as well. From that moment, something has radically changed in our ability to relate to God. By commending his human spirit into the Father's care, he repairs the breach between God and humanity that opened at the moment of Adam's fall from grace. Christ, the New Adam, invites us to be a part of a new humanity, one that once again ᴄan cry out from the depths of its heart, "Abba, Father" (Rom 8:15).

The spirit-wound has a particular effect on men. Because of Adam's fall, they can no longer enter an intimate friendship with God; they have lost contact with themselves and have forgotten how to communicate intimately with others. They have become estranged from their feminine side and when it surfaces are even threatened by it. As a result, men can project that forgotten side onto women and can treat them as objects of pleasure and sexual gratification rather than people created in the image and likeness of God. Significantly, among Jesus's followers—for the most part—only women stood by him to the very end, watching him utter his final words and take his final breath. Significantly, the community of believers upon whom his Holy Spirit descended at Pentecost is often represented in feminine terms. The Church is often referred to as a Spouse of Christ, the Bride of Christ, our holy Mother. The relationship between Jesus and our new humanity can be represented as a reintegration of the masculine and feminine in our human nature. Jesus is the New Adam; Mary, the New Eve. As members of the Church, we are also members of a Mystical Body, with Christ as our Head, and with the Holy Spirit who dwells in our hearts and cries out to the Father on our behalf. When he commends his spirit into his Father's hands, the last breath Jesus takes becomes our first. Vertically, his cross bridges the chasm between God and humanity; horizontally, it bridges the chasm within the human heart and among the hearts of his followers. For men, it signals the healing of the deep yet invisible wound they have been carrying since the Fall.

Conclusion

Catholics believe that the Easter event really happened. We claim that the resurrection is not mere symbol or metaphor, but a factual event. The historical Jesus, we maintain, truly died and truly rose from the dead. His resurrection, however, was not the mere resuscitation of a corpse, but the raising of Jesus's entire person to a higher state of existence, in continuity with his earthly life but now glorified and transformed. For us, there is a fundamental continuity between the earthly Jesus and the Risen Lord. One important feature of this close relationship is the function of Jesus's wounds, all of them clearly visible in his resurrected state but gloriously transformed.

The wounds of the Risen Lord invite us to look into the depths of Christ's paschal mystery. They remind us of the purpose of Jesus's suffering, the love it represents, and its power over death. They also point to the fundamental change that Jesus's passion, death, and resurrection brought about in the lives of his followers. The marks of his passion have become badges of honor and signs of victory. They inspire his followers to follow him in taking up their cross daily and walking in his footsteps. They remind us that Jesus's paschal mystery continues to manifest itself in the lives of his followers. They tell us that he suffered for us and will never abandon us. Because of his love for us, we believe in him, live in him, and follow him wherever his Spirit leads us.

We live in the wounds of the Risen Lord and by his Spirit are empowered to face death with the transforming power of God's love. We live in these wounds because we see in them the promise and hope for our own physical, mental, spiritual, and communal frailties. What is more, we not only live in them, we also look beyond them and live in the hope of showing them one day to the Father and receiving his loving embrace. Catholic men dedicated to the Risen Christ place all their wounds, whatever they may be, in the hands of a loving, compassionate, and merciful God. They do so sure of being healed and ultimately transformed by the power of God's love at work within their hearts. They do so out of love for God and out of God's love for them. They do so because they are seeking healing. They have found that the only way to wholeness is living in the wounds of the Risen Lord. Their challenge lies in responding to the call within their hearts and allowing God's yearning for them to be met by their yearning for God. Such yearning can be satisfied only in the heart of Christ, who yearns for the Father and whose Spirit yearns for us.

Practicing Catholic Male Spirituality

Get up early and watch the sunrise. Get there early enough to witness the first rays breaking through the darkness. Notice that darkness is but an absence of light and that light is the source of all life. As you witness the sun rising, ponder Jesus's victory over death and his rising to new life. In your mind picture the Risen Lord. Stand before him in awe as he displays his transfigured wounds and invites you to place your finger in his hands and side. Bow your head in reverence as he bows his head toward you and beckons you to feel his bruised head. Watch him as he bares his back and shows you the lash marks. Watch him as he manifests his glorified wounds to the world and beckons you to come and rest in him. Rest in the light of the rising sun. Rest in the wounds of the risen and glorified Lord as he embraces your wounds, heals them, and transforms them. Hide your wounds in his. Allow him to touch and elevate you. Witness him rising within your heart, casting out the darkness within you. Watch him as he transforms and divinizes you, readying you for your return to the Father

Prayer to Jesus

Lord, I look to the transfigured wounds of your resurrection as a sign of hope that one day I too might rise. I long for this day and eagerly await its coming. Help me to trust in you Lord. I look at your wounds and find meaning in my suffering. I see them completely transformed by your compassionate life and have come to believe that love is stronger than death, that nothing can separate me from the love of God. Lord, I believe. Help my unbelief. Help me to live my life in fidelity to the gospel message. Help me to live in your risen and glorified wounds. Help me to become a wounded healer whose wounds testify to the transforming power of your love. I love you, Lord. Help me to love you more. Convert me, Lord. Heal me. Glorify me. Make me a true disciple. Lead me along the path of holiness. Make me a saint. Help me to be a man for others. Help me to find God in all things. Make me fully alive so that I may always give glory to you and celebrate the Father's love in all that I think and say and do.

Epilogue

A Manifesto for a
Catholic Spirituality for Men

As we end this exploration, let us summarize the insights and offer a broad (albeit imperfect and tentative) description of its main contours. What follows are the major characteristics of Catholic spirituality for men. It takes the form of a manifesto, because it seeks to set down concisely the general principles of being and acting that should guide Catholic men in their journey of faith and lead them to deeper communion with Christ as members of his Body, the Church.

A Catholic spirituality for men considers not only what men share with everyone else, but also what is particular to them as men. It examines the various dimensions that all human beings share—the physical, psychological, spiritual, and communal—as well as those aspects unique to men. It views these various elements against the backdrop of humanity's being created in the image and likeness of God, the effects of humanity's fall from grace, and the redemptive action of Christ's Incarnation and paschal mystery. It recognizes that there are two complementary ways of being human in the world: the masculine and the feminine. It challenges men to explore the hidden feminine in their lives and, rather than being threatened by it, to integrate it into their identities. It suggests that they open their hearts to the sanctifying work of his Spirit and to participate actively in the life and work of his Mystical Body, the Church. It calls men to live in communion with themselves, others, and all creation.

It invites men on a journey of self-discovery, totally oriented toward others, to communion with God. It requires them to love their families—those of their birth, those born from marriage, and that special one born from above. It implores them to recognize that the search for holiness is a common endeavor and to pray for it.

This spirituality addresses three things that men yearn for deeply: to lead, to provide, and to protect. These desires are hardwired into the male psyche. They stem from the complementarity of the sexes and from multiple factors—biological, psychological, social, spiritual, and cultural. These innate drives provide a context within which men function and derive their sense of legitimacy and self-worth. Blocking men from pursuing these needs can cut them off from their gift of manhood and shut them in a false sense of self that can be difficult, if not impossible, to escape. Men often do not claim their true masculine identity because of deep-seated wounds—those of the father, brother, spirit, and society—caused by humanity's primal fall from grace and the subsequent spiral of hatred, violence, and rage.

A Catholic spirituality for men reveals the remedy for such wounds in the glorified wounds of the Risen Christ. Jesus's scourging reminds us that he is a true brother who always has our backs, never leaving us to face our troubles and hardships alone. His crown of thorns represents men's princely calling, reminding them that the psychological wounds of their darkened minds do not represent their true identities. The wounds of his hands and feet recall the difficulty men face in building things of enduring value, a reminder and acknowledgment that, in the end, only Jesus can empower them to build a lasting city. His pierced side and heart summon men to get in touch with their deepest longings, uniting them with the compassionate heart of Christ, whose blood was poured out for the world's redemption. His hidden wound of lack of breath represents Jesus's impassioned embrace of men's wounded spirits, an embrace that commends them as he himself does to the Father's care.

A Catholic spirituality for men focuses on Jesus, the wounded healer, the risen and glorified Lord. It sees him embracing men's human brokenness and by the power of love transforming their wounds into marks of love's triumph over death. It summons Catholic men to live in the wounds of the Risen Lord. It encourages them to tend the seed of divine love sown in them at Baptism so it will grow within their hearts and radiate throughout their human makeup. It encourages men to share in the sacramental life and mission of the Church. It wants them to glorify God in their bodies (1Cor 6:20), to put on the mind of Christ (1Cor 2:16), to allow the Spirit to intercede for them in their weakness by crying out, "Abba, Father" (Rom 8:15, 26), and to assume an active role in his Body, the Church (1Cor 12:12). It challenges men to place their wounds within those of the Risen Christ so they may be healed and transformed by the power of his love. It extends Jesus's offer of a share in this new life to all who open their hearts and place their trust in him. It offers to bind up men's wounds and heal them. It reminds men that Jesus helps them see the light of truth, acknowledge their feelings, and integrate them with their minds and hearts.

It affirms that Jesus befriends men by sending his Spirit to dwell in their midst and within their hearts. It says that he empowers men to carry his presence to each person they meet. Jesus embraces men's wounds as his own and gives them new meaning in the light of his paschal mystery. As men await the coming of his kingdom, this light helps them peer beneath appearances and recognize the Lord's silent, gentle presence proclaiming its coming while sensing its presence already in their midst. Its light warms men's hearts and although they are wounded, turns them into healers. Its fire lights men's way and marks the journey before them. It leads men to the threshold of the sacred, beyond death. It brings men face-to-face with the mystery of God, letting them glimpse the life beyond. It shows them their place in the brotherhood of men, in the human community, and in the communion of saints. It leads men home, to the place from which they have come, toward which they are journeying, and to which they yearn to return.

In the end, a Catholic spirituality for men is about men becoming themselves in the Catholic faith. It seeks to engage men on every level of their human makeup and to address issues relevant to their experience as men. It challenges them to respond to Jesus's call to discipleship by entering into a personal relationship with Christ lived out in the community of believers. Men play a vital role on every level of Church life. Jesus calls them; the Church needs them; the world needs them. They are called to be strong in faith, vibrant in hope, and deeply in love with God. Their vocation is to integrate their manhood with the call to sanctity and to do this by becoming themselves in the Catholic faith, by being active participants in the life of the Church, and by living every day in the transfigured, glorious wounds of the Risen Lord.

Suggested Reading

Boyer, Mark G. *Biblical Reflections on Male Spirituality*. Collegeville, MN: The Liturgical Press, 1996.

Calvillo, David. *Real Men Pray the Rosary: A Practical Guide to a Powerful Prayer*. Notre Dame, IN: Ave Maria Press, 2013.

Caulfield, Brian. *Man to Man, Dad to Dad: Catholic Faith and Fatherhood*. Boston, MA: Pauline Books and Media, 2013.

Evert, Jason. *Pure Manhood*. San Diego, CA: Catholic Answers Press, 2011.

Gray, Tim, and Curtis Martin. *Boys to Men: The Transforming Power of Virtue*. Steubenville, OH: Emmaus Road Publishing, 2001.

Hain, Randy. *Journey to Heaven: A Road Map for Catholic Men*. Steubenville, OH: Emmaus Road Publishing, 2014.

Lockwood, Robert. *A Guy's Guide to the Good Life: Virtues for Men*. Cincinnati, OH: Servant Books, 2009.

McCoy-Thompson, Steve. *Fuel: Catholic Men, Loving the Faith; A Small Group Guide*. Notre Dame, IN: Ave Maria Press, 2008.

Richards, Fr. Larry. *Be a Man! Becoming the Man God Created You to Be*. San Francisco, CA: Ignatius Press, 2009.

Rohr, Richard. *From Wild Man to Wise Man: Reflections on Male Spirituality*. Cincinnati, OH: St. Anthony Messenger Press, 2005.

_____. *On the Threshold of Transformation: Daily Meditations for Men*. Chicago, IL: Loyola Press, 2010.

Schadt, Devin. *Joseph's Way: 80 Days to Unlocking Your Power as a Father. The Call to Fatherly Greatness: Prayer of Faith*. San Francisco, CA: Ignatius Press, 2014.

Schneider, Matthew. *Spiritually Mentoring Teenage Boys: Personal Dialogue to Make Young Saints*. Mission Network Programs USA, Inc., 2014.

Sri, Edward. *Men, Women and the Mystery of Love: Practical Insights from John Paul II's* Love and Responsibility. Cincinnati, OH: Servant Books, 2007.

Sullivan, Tim, and Bill Bawden. *Signposts: How to be a Catholic Man in the World Today.* Jamesville, MD: The Word Among Us Press, 1999.

Zimmerer, Jared. *Man Up! Becoming the New Catholic Renaissance Man.* Waterford, MI: Bezalel Books, 2014.

Ziolkowski, Peter. *Discipleship for Catholic Men: Embracing God's Plan for Our Life.* Overland Park, KS: *National Fellowship of Catholic Men,* 2007.

NEW CITY PRESS
Hyde Park, New York

New City Press is one of more than 20 publishing houses sponsored by the Focolare, a movement founded by Chiara Lubich to help bring about the realization of Jesus' prayer: "That all may be one" (John 17:21). In view of that goal, New City Press publishes books and resources that enrich the lives of people and help all to strive toward the unity of the entire human family. We are a member of the Association of Catholic Publishers.

Other books by Fr. Dennis Billy published by NCP

Living in the Gap—Religious Life and the Call to Communion, Second Edition
978-1-56548-583-9 $13.95

The book wishes to raise awareness of the importance of the vocation to the consecrated life in the life of Church and to help religious in their efforts towards the new evangelization.

The Mystery of the Eucharist—Voices from the Saints and Mystics
978-1-56548-530-3 $24.95

This book examines the Eucharistic teaching and contribution of twenty-six saints and mystics from the church's past including John Paul II, St. John Damascene, Thomas Merton, Teresa of Calcutta and Chiara Lubich.

The Beauty of the Eucharist—Voices from the Church Fathers
978-1-56548-328-6 $17.95

This book examines what some of the most prominent voices of Christianity's distant past have taught about the Eucharist including Ambrose, Basil the Great, Gregory of Nyssa, John Chrysostom, Jerome, and Augustine of Hippo.

Gospel Joy—Pope Francis and the New Evangelization 978-1-56548-566-2 $11.95

This book examines the central elements of Francis' vision of the Church as it sets out to preach the gospel to people of every nation and every walk of life.

Tending The Mustard Seed—Living the Faith in Today's World
978-1-56548-475-7 $11.95

This book contains powerful reflections on faith in the life of the disciple of Christ, with accompanying reflection questions, and can be an excellent vehicle for prayer and study groups.

Mary in 3-D—Icon of Discipleship, Doctrine, and Devotion 978-1-56548-603-4 $9.95

Presents devotion to the sacred icon of Our Mother of Perpetual Help, in the larger theological and spiritual context of the church's general Marian teaching.